MW01075270

trees amongst GRAVES

ANDREW SISK

Palmetto Publishing Group
Charleston, SC

Trees Amongst Graves
Copyright © 2019 by Andrew Sisk

First Edition

Printed in the United States

ISBN 13: 9781641114745
ISBN-10: 1641114746

My hope and heart for this book is to call people to true life. To call those who are truly living to bring others along with them. As you are reading this, I want it to be remembered and known that my words are not God's words. His words are eternal, and if my words are not aligned with His they are useless, but if they are aligned they are potent and powerful. I encourage you take everything said and compare it to the word of God (Holy Bible) and see if it aligns with His word. His word gives life, and I hope you are encouraged and blessed by reading this.

-Andrew Sisk

Special thanks to my mother Christianna Sisk for editing and supporting.

TABLE OF CONTENTS

TREES
AMONGST
GRAVES

Chapter 1

GRAVES

Death is weird. No one really likes death, but it seems to be the inescapable fate that we all face. Nothing draws our undivided attention, or penetrates our soul quite the way death does. To dwell on it only leads to inevitable depression, or a true wake up call. I am sure many of you who may find the time to read this book have experienced death of some sort in your lifetime. I do not want to stir up bad memories or broken emotions, but to have you recall the intentionality of those times.

Recently, two dear friends of mine tragically passed away in two separate car accidents. Both of the accidents happened within a month of each other. Their names were Taylor and Amelia, and both of them are easily some of the most remarkable people you could ever meet. They were dear friends of mine in college, and because we all attended such a small school it was as if the whole community lost a member of our family. They were so kind, so sweet, connected with people so easily, and they are dearly missed. When they passed it was one of the strangest times of my life, seeing what death could do to a whole community. It was amazing to see the impact their lives, and the end of those lives had on the world around us. Amelia and Taylor were valued by many, and losing them tore the hearts of myself and those around me.

> "Better to spend your time at funerals than at parties. After all, everyone dies— so the living should take this to heart." Ecclesiastes 7:2 (NLT)

When our dear loved ones passed on it consumed our souls, hearts, and minds with grief. Their deaths hurled the community into an examination of this life. This is the intentionality I was talking about. Even though there was an extreme anguish felt; it pulled out of us something beautiful. A deeper affection for the ones surrounding us, our family, friends, lovers, and even in our acquaintances. We all found a new appreciation and respect for one another. We checked up on one another, we were sure to tell the ones around us we loved them. We intentionally loved.

Wounded by the loss of two wonderful souls, I can honestly say that through this tragedy it awakened us to attention. A wake up call that reminded us this life is but a vapor. Here today, gone tomorrow. Life is so fragile, and unfortunately sometimes the only way to call some to really live life to the fullest is through the death of something of value.

Although Amelia and Taylor moved on from this life, it is safe to say, the time they spent here on earth they truly were alive. They were not just physically alive, but spiritually alive, which is more than you can say for many who are still living today. As I reflect on their death, I feel it is only right to take this opportunity to call others to live a life similar to the way these girls did, and that is a life full of true life.

You see, death is very diverse, and it is not limited to the end of someone's physical life, but it can take many forms. We all have heard the phrase "Every man dies. Not every man really lives." (William Wallace). Death is not just lowering someone six feet underground, but it can creep it's way in among the living. Death can appear in the young man who is the life of the party, but goes home and feels so alone and empty within. Death can appear in a broken woman who has been scarred by life, and no matter the effort or strength put in to find the joy she so longs for, she cannot seem to grasp it. Death can be a father who provides everything for his family out of obligation rather than love. Death can be the young generation that has everything from the highest pleasures to the money to buy an island, but no concern for the poor or the needy, and is self obsessed.

To put it plainly, death is alive and active all around us. It is on the move in our world today as we know it. You or dearly loved ones can be the very ones who are already in their graves. I am not talking about a physical death, but spiritual. Oh, how many people walk this earth with an emptiness that cannot be filled. So many are walking, moving, and breathing headstones. Just because you have breath within your lungs does not mean you have life within your spirit.

Maybe you who are reading this can feel the tugging on your heart that you yourself are deep within your own grave. You are gasping for air, and if you had a gravestone it would say: "Here lies (enter name), I sure know how to bury away my hurts and troubles, I bring no joy or energy to life, I go to work dazed, longing for it to be over. I go home and I never am satisfied with how life is. I am so broken within, because I am consumed with myself and my wants and my needs. I have no intention to relieve the pain of others when I myself have hurts too deep to cure."

We all know those people. Shoot, maybe you are that person. Let's call them grave diggers, because day by day they dig deeper and deeper into death. Let's not get it twisted, I myself have been a grave digger, and If I am not careful, it is a quick trap to fall into the death that so easily entangles our souls while we still live.

Maybe you want to know, am I a grave digger? Maybe you already know you are. I want to go through 3 characteristics that appear in your common grave digger and you can decide where you stand.

BURIED IN DARKNESS

After someone passes away, not so long after we have a burial for them. We take their bodies and begin to cover them with 6 feet of dirt. Have you ever felt buried? I mean not physically but mentally, emotionally, or spiritually? I can imagine some of you feel buried in all three areas of you life, but instead of dirt you feel buried in other things such as chaos, fear, and shame. Maybe anxiousness covers you and you constantly feel the weight of it pouring over the top of you. Even if I did not mention what you feel buried in, it still has the same feeling. It's heavy, restricting, and it feels like to much to bare. If you are a human being you probably have felt like this one time or another, but there are some who live life like this. They constantly are weighed down. This is an exhausting place to live from, and my heart goes out to those who can not seem to find relief on any side.

If that is not depressing enough to be buried under the weight of all that dirt; being buried implies that you are hidden from light. That is why I called this section buried in darkness. Not only do you feel the weight of all these things, you have no light to guide you out of the situation you are in.

Without light, it is impossible to have any sense of direction. Light reveals things that are happening around you, so that you may find the right and correct path. Light not only reveals truth, light has a way of being refreshing. There is nothing quite like sunlight after a long winter. Sunlight is proven to cause your brain to be attentive, have better memory, and raise energy levels. I have heard it once said that 15 minutes of sunlight has the same effect as drinking one cup of coffee. The sad thing is that everything light does, darkness does the opposite. Many people are buried underneath the weight of this life, and they have no light in their life... Some people have been in darkness so long they have become accustomed to it that it feels natural to be in darkness. It feels so natural that they call it light even though it is truly darkness.

Maybe you are that person. You are so used to being weighed down that you do not know what it feels like to be free of burdens. A lot of people are convinced they are free, but in reality they are in deep bondage. The Bible says a lot about this.

> "But when your eye is unhealthy, your whole body is filled with darkness. And if the light you think you have is actually darkness, how deep that darkness is!" Matthew 6:23 NLT

> "So there is no justice among us, and we know nothing about right living. We look for light but find only darkness. We look for bright skies but walk in gloom. We grope like the blind along a wall, feeling our way like people without eyes. Even at brightest noontime, we stumble as though it were dark. Among the living, we are like the dead." Isaiah 59:9-10 NLT

I am not here to shame you if you feel this way. I have often felt this way and lived life like this. Rather, I am here to shed some light on the state you may be in. I am here to shed some truth, because the truth sets men and women free. The only way to be released from bondage is to know you are actually in bondage. One of the biggest tactics of satan is to keep people oblivious, but God reveals things to heal them. He does not reveal our struggles or flaws to shame us, but rather to liberate us.

Here is the truth: Jesus is the light of the world that carries our burdens.

> "Jesus spoke to the people once more and said, 'I am the light of the world. If you follow me, you won't have to walk in darkness, because you will have the light that leads to life.'" John 8:12 NLT

> "This is the message we heard from Jesus and now declare to you: God is light, and there is no darkness in him at all." 1 John 1:5 NLT

I find it interesting that Jesus claims to be the light of the world in John 8, right after the story of the woman caught in the act of adultery. I encourage you to read it. In this story there was a woman caught in the act of adultery and many religious leaders wanted to stone her. They wanted to bury her underneath a pile of rocks. I think today those rocks can represent shame, guilt that many people want to throw on top of us. Jesus resolves the situation and the women goes free, and He does not condemn her by burying her under more rocks.

I tell you this, because many of you may feel buried underneath the opinions of others. You may feel condemned by others, but Jesus has not come to condemn, or have you be squashed underneath your own mistakes. Instead, He came so that you do not have to carry the weight of the world on your shoulders. He wants to carry it for you.

> "Then Jesus said, 'Come to me, all of you who are weary and carry heavy burdens, and I will give you rest. Take my yoke upon you. Let me teach you, because I am humble and gentle at heart, and you will find rest for your souls. For my yoke is easy to bear, and the burden I give you is **light**.'" Matthew 11:28-30 NLT

He wants to carry your burdens so badly He was crucified, and buried so that He could come to you while you were buried in darkness. He rose again so that He may lift you out of the dirt as well. He rose again so you may see the light of day and carry the light in you. Your burden no longer is your sin, shame, and heaviness of life. Your burden is to receive the light and see the truth that He has carried your burdens for you. So keep believing He has taken it all from your shoulders and put it on Himself.

My prayer for those who feel buried, weighted down and exhausted by life would come the truth they do not have to be buried any longer. May you receive rest from the burdens you have carried for so long. I leave you with this verse.

> "Feed the hungry, and help those in trouble. Then your light will shine out from the darkness, and the darkness around you will be as bright as noon. The Lord will guide you continually, giving you water when you are dry and restoring your strength. You will be like a well-watered garden, like an ever-flowing spring." Isaiah 58:10-11 NLT

SMELLY (AROMA OF DEATH)

I am not much of a hunter, and do you want to know what keeps me away from hunting the most? It is not because

I am an avid animal lover, but rather the thought of gutting something after I have shot it just disgusts me. I have heard to many horror stories of the rancid smell of something that has been dead for a long period of time. Yeah no thanks fam. I will stick to those arcade hunting games for now.

The point I am trying to make is that things are dead have a smell to them, and it is not pleasant. Have you ever been around someone who just flat out smells bad? It is hard to be around them, even if they have a sense of humor or are amazing all other ways.

I have an embarrassing story, one time I was working in a factory that produced thousands of chairs a day. We were working hard and there was no stopping. Another gal and I were working on putting the pieces from one bin to another, and I was grinding hard. Unfortunately I forgot to put on deodorant that day.... and though I was working hard and getting a lot done, my coworker eventually could not handle the smell of body odor any longer. She went and got my boss to tell me. I was embarrassed, but I was thankful they told me so I could do something about it, because regardless of what I produced work wise my stench made me unbearable to be around.

I think people live this life with a stench.. their spirit has made them hard to be around.. It comes from their soul being dead on the inside. Whatever is it going on the inside of us eventually comes out whether it be good or bad.

> "Make a tree good and its fruit will be good, or make a tree bad and its fruit will be bad, for a tree is recognized by its fruit. You brood of vipers, how can you who are evil say anything good? For the mouth speaks what the heart is full of. A good man brings good things out of the good stored up in him, and an evil man brings evil things out of the evil stored up in him." Matthew 12:33-35 NIV

Who we are speaks in more ways then just words. Our essence and the way we carry ourselves has an aroma that comes with us when we walk into a room, and If we have the things of death hidden in our heart, we carry it with us. If bitterness is in our hearts it is going to manifest itself in our lives through lack of trust, brokenness, and abrasive behavior. People with discernment have a way of sniffing out if a person is bad news or not. Mom's are pretty good at this, It is called a mother's intuition, like smell though it is unseen it can still be sensed.

What does your aroma bring? Does it bring peace or uneasiness to the situation? The aroma you have says a lot about what is going on on the inside. I encourage you to look inside yourself and see what is going on in you that is causing you to now have a pleasing aroma. God wants you to have an aroma that draws people near to see of the goodness of God burning within you like a candle.

> "For we are to God the pleasing aroma of Christ among those who are being saved and those who are perishing." 2 Corinthians 2:15 NIV

JESUS DOES NOT WANT YOU TO LIVE IN DEATH

If you are coming to the realization that you are in the place of spiritual death, the good news is that does not have to be your final destination. You do not have to be buried in darkness, with a foul smelling spirit. You can be risen from the dead just like Jesus was, and have His spirit come and live within you. Jesus wants to uncover you so that you might discover who you were made to be! Death wasn't designed for you. You are designed to live. The Good news is if you know someone who is dead now spiritually it does not mean they have to stay that way. There is hope and our hope comes from a Tree.

Chapter 2

TREES

So lets talk about the living. The ones not in their graves, but the ones that have a heart beat inside of them. Let's refer to these people as trees. The reason why is because all throughout grade school it felt like the fact that trees are actually a living species kept being brought up, and from the third grade on it has stuck with me, so we are sticking with it. I also think for the most part we as human beings enjoy the sight of trees, and we love their presence. I have never heard anyone say, "wow, I really love a barren land without any trees." That is usually not our cup of tea, but show someone a beautiful mountain range full of lush trees it tends to spark an awe in us. As I used to drive through Yellowstone National Park on my way back to school the livelihood of the trees on those mountain passes stirred an appreciation for the parts of the earth that can truly be so breathtaking.

A place where trees are is usually a sign of vibrant pure life, from jungles to rainforests, where creatures of all sorts find their homes. Even just a tree in your backyard that you would climb up as a child, for whatever reason, gave you a sense of peace and freedom. Trees are landscape changers, a breath of fresh air, a beauty to behold, and a joy to so many, yet they can be taken for granted.

I think we all know people like that. People that when they come into the room the atmosphere changes completely. They are a breath of fresh air, and bring joy to others. These people can turn everyone from having a very dull moment, to having a memorable moment. We all have those people, that the thought of getting to hang out with them makes us giddy inside like small children at recess. They can bring joy to a broken room, a sense of hope in a world that seems hopeless, and love where love seems to be lost. Just their presence brings a calmness to the storm that is surrounding so many. These people are so rare, so precious, such a gift to this world and they take after their Creator. They are like Him, because they abide in Him.

In John Chapter 15, Jesus says He is the vine, and if we abide (remain in relationship with) in Him we are like branches that produce good fruit. The good fruit He is talking about is not like apples or oranges, but it is our lives full of spiritual fruit such as love, joy, patience, along with other things. All characteristics that come from the author and creator of all things. If we remain in Jesus, we are going to produce these things in our life, because He is in us and He is these things.

Jesus is love. "For anyone who does not love does not know God for God is love." 1 John 4:8-9 (NIV).

Jesus is joy. Luke Chapter 1 talks about Jesus in the womb of His mother, Mary, and Mary was going to visit Elizabeth who was pregnant with John the Baptist. As soon as Elizabeth entered the room the baby in her womb (John the Baptist) jumped with joy in her belly, because of who Mary was carrying in her womb (Jesus).

What kind of immense and powerful joy is this where not even a fully formed child in a womb can cause another child in a separate womb to sense His presence and rejoice? If Jesus as a fetus can cause this amount of joy, what do you think the resurrected King Jesus who holds all the stars in place can do in your life?

In other words, the seed form of Jesus caused an extreme amount of joy, but the seed is always the beginning and it grows into something larger and bigger producing even more seeds. Jesus wants to increase your joy exponentially to have no end and to plant seeds of joy in others lives as well. We will take about this later in the book.

Jesus is patient. From the time He was taken back up into heaven, He has been patiently waiting to make His return. He has been patiently waiting to take for Himself those who have devoted themselves to Him. This would be like an engaged couple who are so desperately in love with each other, and all the desire in their heart is just to get married. They would love to jump the gun, but they continue to wait for each other in order for the timing to be right, and for all the arrangements to be put into order. Jesus is doing the same thing, and holding back from what is rightfully His; in order that many more who do not know Him yet can come to know Him. He does this so they too can come with Him into eternal life. His patience shows His kindness to sinners who would be in hell if He returned right now, and His patience shows just how good He is to allow the same sinners some more time that they might make it to heaven as well.

If we produce the same type of love, joy, and patience in our life the way Jesus does, then it will be sign to us, and to others we are truly alive. It will be a sign to us we are "trees" that are among the graves.

I want to talk more about what it means to be a tree. Therefore; the same way I discussed some characteristics of those in the grave, I will also point out a few characteristics of "trees"; the people who have true life.

PLANTED (FAITH)

First things first, trees are planted. The foundation of people being full of life is they themselves are planted. By planted I mean they are secure, they remain still, firm, and set in the assurance they have through faith in God. They are not easily shaken by what life throws their way, because they have an assurance in Who they are planted on and in.

> "Anyone who listens to my teaching follows it is wise, like a person who builds a house on solid rock.Though the rain comes in torrents and the floodwaters rise and the winds beat against that house, it won't collapse because it is built on bedrock." Matthew 7:24-25

People who are planted on what God has said are like trees planted in solid ground that is not easily moved. Have you ever met anyone who has really been through it? I mean really, really been through it? Yet their soul is not shaken one bit, and all you can think is, how are they so strong and calm right now? They should be weeping, confused, afraid, depressed, and angry, but yet they remain still and calm.

I am willing to bet everyone one of us have come across hard times in this life that has brought us to our knees. It is inevitable on this earth. Many times I have gone through difficult seasons, and all I desire within is that I was more stable. I wish through all things, no matter what life could muster up, I still would be secure. I desire that I would not be shaken, and that I would be PLANTED in the truths of who Jesus is. The difference between those who are planted and those who are thrown around like a rag doll when the rain and wind comes, is the confidence they have within that God is good. A confidence that God is for them and not against them. A confidence that "God works all things for good for those who love him." Romans 8:28 (NIV).

People who are planted are not shaken by lack of resources, but they trust that God is a provider in all times. If God can bring Elijah food by sending him ravens in the desert in 1 Kings Chapter 17, then surely God can pay that bill you need to be paid by the end of the month. Surely, He can provide a way out of any stronghold. Surely, He will provide a spouse that will be good to you. Surely, God will provide for you. Surely He can can provide the strength you need to endure any season.

It's who He is, Jehovah Jireh. Providing is what He does.

I myself can be shaken, and it really shows that I need to grow in my own personal trust and assurance in God. I have been known to put my trust, hope, and self worth in what others think of me. I want to be liked. I want to be loved. I want to be special to someone. These are all pretty normal, but it is so dangerous to place my confidence in these things that are not God, because these things can be shaken. We must put our trust in an unshakable God. The moment the people I rely on to love me deeply do not show me the love I think I should be receiving, I begin to question my self worth. You know what would solve this problem? If I had an unshakeable and unbreakable faith in the love of Jesus, and how truly precious I am to Him.

If I truly believed that even death could not separate His love from me, my soul would rest in the assurance of love I have in Him. If I truly believed the grave could not contain His love for me, I would have the joy of being loved all throughout my days. If I truly believed He was not afraid to step from all majesty and power to put on skin and bones and live among us to love us, and if I truly believed He looked to the cross, an excruciating shameful death, and still pressed on in order to win my heart, then I would not be in shambles when others fail to love me perfectly. In fact, I would not even need these others people to love me, as long as I had Christ's love.

> "The Lord is my Shepherd I shall not want." Psalm 23:1

God has grown me to trust in His love more and more, but I still want to grow deeper in my trust so nothing can shake me.

You see, true trees are planted and they have a childlike faith when it comes to the things that God has said. They don't question, even if all the surrounding circumstances do no match up; they know deep within their being, God's love will come through again and again. Though it may be unseen, it is more solid than the ground we stand on. It is as sure as the next breath we take that God is for us.

> "God is our refuge and strength, an ever-present help in trouble. Therefore we will not fear, though the earth give way and the mountains fall into the heart of the sea, though its waters roar and foam and the mountains quake with their surging.

He says, "Be still, and know that I am God; I will be exalted among the nations, I will be exalted in the earth." Psalm 46:1-3, 10 NIV

Trees are the mothers who tell us everything is going to be okay after a rough day at school, because Jesus is still in control. Trees are those people who have experienced such loss, but yet they still proclaim the goodness of God. They don't wallow in self-pity when life gets hard, but they remain calm and at peace through all seasons. Trees are the spouses that hold their significant other close in the midst of financial struggles, in the midst of loss, and in the midst of attack against their families. They are a stronghold for those who are in need and feel lost, and knocked down by life. Maybe you run to these trees when you are afraid, or maybe you are the tree people run to when they are afraid, because they know you are not easily swayed by life's storms. These people provide the comfort of shade in the midst of the hot sun. (Heat of life)

"Yet when planted, it grows and becomes the largest of all garden plants, with such big branches that the birds can perch in its shade." Mark 4:32 NIV

People who are planted are not moved by fear, but rather stand firm on faith. Fear has no hold on them. Fear can taunt loudly, and crash hard like the waves of the sea, but even still planted people are not moved. Fear is actually an attribute of those who are in the grave, because fear will cripple you from the life you truly are designed to live. Fear will cause strife when there is no need for any. Fear is illegitimate, and you will never live life experiencing it's fullness if you are run by fear.

Fear will hold you from love and freedom. Fear will keep you from confidence, and will keep you from your purpose and destiny. Fear will keep you from moments that make a memory that lasts a lifetime. Fear is from satan, and to abide in fear is to believe the lies of the devil over the truth of what God has said.

Assurance on the other hand is faith, and confidence in God. Being planted in faith does the exact opposite of fear. Those who are planted in Christ and his words have not been given a spirit of fear, but of love and a sound mind. My prayer is that any of who are reading this would have fear completely broken from your life, and that you would have the security in an unshakeable God. My hope is that you would be planted through every storm, standing firm in every obstacle, unbroken in every nightmare, and in every trial you remain planted in the love of the Father.

Let it be known that in times of being shaken, God is shaking that things out of your life that can be shaken, so that you will rest on the unshakable Father.

PHOTOSYNTHESIS

Secondly, trees do something very important for our environment. They create oxygen through the process of photosynthesis. Here is a small science lesson from someone who barely passed all of his science classes through school, but bear with me as I try to make a point. We as humans, by breathing, take in oxygen and then exhale carbon dioxide. Trees then take in the carbon dioxide from the atmosphere and from the energy the sun provides, takes the carbon dioxide and joins it with water, then releasing oxygen back into the atmosphere for us humans to survive on. If it was not for the trees we would be living in an atmosphere filled with carbon dioxide, and that is well, toxic.

We would not be able to survive, because the large amounts of carbon dioxide are not good for us. Too much can cause shortness of breath, fatigue, and could lead to death, and we as humans breathe that stuff out with every breath we take! Most of us do not even realize we breathe out chemicals that could be toxic and detrimental to all other human life. Kind of the same way we do not always realize some of our behaviors are toxic to others around us. We push out toxins into the spiritual atmosphere with our actions and words.Thankfully, we have trees that transform the toxins from the air and create oxygen, there are people who can transform toxic spiritual atmospheres to a breath of fresh air.

The people who are 'Trees' are spiritual atmosphere changers. They can take any situation, no matter the toxicity of it and bring forth something life bringing. These people can take on the hurts, the gossip, the insults, the curses, the abuse, and all the deep harmful things this earth has to offer, and digest all of it and return not more harmful behaviors, but transform them into love, peace, unity, encouragement, and a sense of hope.

For example, have you heard of the Charleston church shooting? A 21 year old white male, filled with hate for African Americans and Christians went and took the lives of 9 people in a South Carolina church back in 2015. Truly a devastating act filled with such hate, racism, bigotry, wickedness, and corruption. You would think such a hateful act would only stir up anger and revenge in the families that lost the lives of their loved ones. Actually, that is not what happened at all. I would recommend you see it for yourself what these people did in return to the one who persecuted them. It is 4 minutes long, but it is such a powerful video. You can watch it on YouTube: shooting victims kin: i forgive you.

Powerful isn't it? If you didn't watch it, long story short, at the hearing of the murderer, the family of the victims of the lives he took were there and they were telling him they forgive him. They invited him to a Bible study with open arms. They were hoping he would find the love of God. Are you kidding me? How? Where? Where do they get this kind of love and strength to look in the eyes of the one who hurt you so deeply, and be able to say I forgive you, and then embrace them? These people are the epitome of "trees". They took in hurt and returned forgiveness, grace, and love.

Where did these people learn this from? They learned it from Jesus. Imagine Jesus, hanging on a cross, after being beaten, spit on, mocked, punched, stripped naked, after being whipped 39 times with a cat of nine tails. Imagine nails hammered into His feet and hands, hanging on a tree, thirsty, and abandoned. Bearing all the weight of the history and sin of mankind. Every ounce of guilt and penalty was placed on Him, all the while being insulted by the ones He came to die for, and what was His response? Jesus should have said, "I'm out of here, these suckers deserve condemnation." But no..

He remained and Jesus said, "Father forgive them, they know not what they do." This is unheard of love. Love that transcends understanding. Love that cannot be quenched. Love that is as demanding as the grave. Love that cannot be washed away, and love that will stand until the end of time.

Jesus was the first person to perform spiritual photosynthesis. He took in all of our toxic and sinful behaviors on Himself. He digested it and died, but from His death won victory over sin, and rose again. Not to bring revenge, but to bring love to you and I. He took our hate, and gave forgiveness, He took our insults, and returned honor to us.

> "God made him who had no sin to be sin for us, so that in him we might become the righteousness of God." 2 Corinthians 5:21 NIV

The ultimate photosynthesis. Wow... I love Jesus, and I am so thankful He did that for you and I. I cannot help but want to honor Him, and be just like Him.

"Trees" are imitators of Christ, and the Charleston church community are great examples. You can do the same. When you go to work, and the atmosphere is filled with gossip about another coworker, you can interject and defend that person with honor. When someone is speaking badly on your name, you can return love back to them. When discouragement is in the room, you can be the one that brings encouragement to others. When Satan tries to throw curses your way, you can rest in the fact God is going to take that curse and turn it into a blessing. The same way He absorbed the curse of death, and brought forth eternal life through it. You are His child and the apple does not fall far from the tree.

SAP

That brings me to the last characteristic of a tree that I am going to talk about. They have sap. You know that terrible sticky stuff you used to get on your hands and arms when you would climb trees as a kid? Yeah that stuff. I am not saying those that are truly living are sticky and annoying, but I think most of us have never really stopped to think of the true purpose of sap for a tree. Sap is like the blood of a tree. Sap is the trees form of protection, and internal healing when the tree is wounded. When a tree is wounded by storms, animals, insects, or flying objects it releases sap to cover the wound to protect it from being further infected, and eventually bring healing to the tree. Trees have their own natural internal healing source, ready to go whenever a wound may take place.

Same thing goes for people who are "trees". Trees have no way to control whether or not a storm may come through and take off a chunk of bark, or whether a careless lawn mower cuts them with a weed wacker in three different places. It is the same for us as people while we are on this earth. We can not always avoid all the pain that may come our way, nor stop all the storms of life from coming unannounced. We can not always stop careless people from leaving a dent in our hearts, and sometimes we can not even stop ourselves from afflicting ourselves with hurts. Life's pain is guaranteed, and no one is immune to it. What shall we do with this then? If we are bound to be wounded at some point, what is going to separate those who survive and overcome versus those who die from it? The answer is the internal source of healing. The sap. You can be wounded, but does not have to be the end of you.

"But we have this treasure in jars of clay to show that this all-surpassing power is from God and not from us. We are hard pressed on every side, but not crushed; perplexed, but not in despair; persecuted, but not abandoned; struck down, but not destroyed." 2 Corinthians 4:7-9 NIV

I would compare sap to being similar to the Spirit of Christ in us. We have His blood flowing through us, His blood that purchased our healing on the cross is the sap to our souls. The writer of 2 Corinthians, Paul, does not disregard the hardships of life, but he realizes because of Christ who is living inside of him, he can endure all things. Not just endure but be made whole, and have victory. He had an assurance that he and his partners would survive and be healed from all that life threw at them.

Have you ever been through a heart break? There is nothing quite like a heart wound. It makes you feel weak, tired, helpless, and can even make you feel worthless. In my short life I have gone through a few heartbreaks; some minor and some major. I will tell you about two of them. One when I did not have Christ in my life and the other when I did have Christ in my life.

When I was 17 I was convinced I was in love with a girl in my high school. I was foolish, but nonetheless convinced she was the one. I do not want to get into the details, but it ended up not working out, and it turned she had a crush on my fellow close friend. There was a lot that went into it, but it destroyed me. Yeah yeah, make fun of me for my dramatic high school self, but it was a reality that I was broken. My heart hurt so deeply, but I had nothing within me that could bring healing to it. I would try outside sources, like parties, other girls, or thrills. None of it truly worked; they were like band aids that would fall off instantly. I would listen to sad songs, and walk around school depressed. All very dramatic.

Long story short it took me two years to finally stop thinking about it. Two years! It was a 2 month relationship. Wow, as I write about it I feel more pathetic then before. Why did it take so long to be mended from that? The reason why is I didn't allow Christ to have the hurts of my heart. I believed in other things to bring healing, but it never came. I made myself a victim of my wounds, and I allowed it to be infected causing much more pain then there needed to be. Who knew a dumb high school crush could bring this much hurt? That is the problem, it shouldn't have, but I allowed it to become infected and strike sickness and grief into my soul.

Fast forward to when Christ was living in me. I spoke of it in the first Chapter, when two of my friends lost their lives in car accidents. It was horrible, and my heart hurt so deeply for the loss of my friends, and for the families who lost their daughters, but something was different this time, I never became the victim. I never became angry, or bitter. It is not because I did not care about them; I loved both of them dearly, but I had an internal sap. I had The love and comfort of Christ Jesus oozing from my soul where life had cut deep into. Instead of broken, I felt inspired to be there for others, to love more deeply, and to love now while I still had the chance. It has been about 7 months since their deaths, and though I mourn I can think back about my loss and I can rejoice in the times I got to spend with them. I can rejoice, because I know they are dancing, praising Jesus and shouting His glory in perfect peace.

How is it a minor crush broke me for two years, but the death of friends built me stronger in just a few months? It is the sap. The Holy Spirit doing a mighty work of healing, comforting and defending from further damage then there needed to be.

I know we all mourn differently, and I am not saying just because you have Jesus in your life it is not okay to feel pain or grief. All that I am trying to say is having the Holy Spirit of Christ should have you mourn and hurt differently then everyone else. You mourn with hope. You know it shall pass, and you do not become the victim of what has hurt you. In fact the pain you feel within now has a purpose of making you more Christlike. The sap of the tree does not allow wound to become the death of it.

Some of you have hurts that I can not even begin to understand, but know this, God is the ultimate healer. He brings total restoration to those who trust in Him, and your hurts do not have to be the end of you. Some of you may be going through heart break right now, but my advice is give Christ your wounded heart and allow Him to cover it in His healing sap His Holy Spirit. Some of you have been wounded sexually, physically, emotionally, and spiritually, but I want you to know you can trust Jesus with the pain. He is gentle and kind at heart, He will kiss your wounds and has the power to completely restore all that is lost. That is my prayer for you in Jesus name!

Also I pray that all of you reading this would allow this supernatural healing rest inside of your soul and when life hurts you, the healing will just ooze from within, rather than looking for false healing to come from outside sources.

Chapter 3

BECOMING

So how do we become these awesome people? Who are so secure in what God has spoken, able to change atmospheres just with our presence, and able to find healing from the inside. It seems pretty daunting, and even as I write about this I do not always have the characteristics of a tree. I am not always secure in what God says about me or my situation. Sometimes I add to the negative smell to an atmosphere, and I will be honest, sometimes I look for outside sources to heal my wounds. I do desire to have all of the characteristics of a tree, and I want to be an awesome person right now. I want the end result of the tree, but God is telling me that the seed must be planted for the tree to reach full bloom. It is going to be a process.

That should be refreshing for each and every one of us who are broken, messed up, and still have issues, because, "He who began a good work in us will bring it unto completion" (Philippians 1:6). All it takes is a seed to be planted, and through the process, we can eventually become the person who is fully alive. So take heart, you people who feel like they are not quite there yet, and trust the process. You may just be a small size mustard seed, but one day you will become a full grown, powerful, beautiful tree, producing fruit and shade for those around you.

SEED

The first thing you need to start this process of becoming a tree, is the seed. Matthew Chapter 13 says that the seed that is planted is the "word" of God. "Word" is just another fancy way of saying Jesus. It is because Christ is the fulfillment of the word of God. He is the complete living embodiment of the word of God. He lived out all of the law of the Old Testament perfectly. He met every requirement in the Old Testament. All the small laws and the big ones, and the point of the law: Love, mercy, and justice.

When Jesus died on the cross, He displayed His immense love for us. Christ pouring himself out on our behalf fulfilled the requirement of love that we as humans have failed to follow. "No greater love than this, to lay your life down for your friends" John 15:13, and that is what Christ did for you and I. This love is so extravagant, and hard to comprehend. Could you imagine actually laying your life down for someone? Put yourself in that position, or in a situation where it's your life or the life of someone else. What would you do? If it was your Mom you would maybe think about dying for her survival, but what if it was someone who hates and rejects everything that you are? Would you die for them? I highly doubt it, but Christ did this for us.

> "God demonstrates his love for us while
> we were still sinners, Christ died for us."
> Romans 5:8

I heard the Spirit of the Lord tell me that "He died for dust". In the story of creation when God formed man, He formed him from the dust of the earth. Dust is what we were before God got involved. Dust does not have much value, and dust is dirty. What great love is this that a creator would die for dust. Let me explain, God died for us when we were nothing, He died for us when we were dirty. So many of us feel like we have to clean ourselves up and become something before God will love us. Nope! God sacrificially love us while we were messed up, depressed, broken, addicted, and filthy.

He displays this on the cross to show our true identity as loved! When we know who we are we then become something.

I say this a lot in my sermons on Sunday mornings, but man, if Christ loved us enough to die for us people who make horrible mistakes, how much more do you think He rejoices in living for us and pouring His love out on us. He already finished the hard part.

His love displayed on the cross gave mercy to us sinners, by taking on our punishment, and also serving justice, because someone had to pay for the wages of sin. I am forever grateful that Christ did that on our behalf. By Him doing all of this He planted a seed in my heart. He planted the seed of love in my heart. He planted the seed of forgiveness in my heart. He planted the seed of joy in my heart. He planted the seed of mercy in my heart, and He planted life. All in the hope that one day I might become a tree that produces the same thing for others around me. He did not just do that for me, but for all of mankind. Christ is the seed that was planted in us, to begin the process of becoming a tree, and that brings us to the next thing that is vital for us growing into trees. The soil.

SOIL

The seed is only as effective as the soil, for without good soil, the seed goes to waste. Do not get me wrong the seed is good, but the soil determines it's growth. Soil is the representation of the state of our heart, and in order for a seed to grow it has to be in good soil. In other words the state of your heart can really prohibit or exhibit all that God is trying to plant and grow inside of you. Again, Matthew 13 talks about seeds that were planted on different soils. In other words, the life of Jesus being told to different people, and how they receive it. Each of us have a heart of our own, and we all receive things differently. Jesus describes these different soils, and explains the different outcome of each seed. There is the seed that was planted, but birds came and stole it (hearts that give power to Satan), the seed that was planted in a rocky place (hard hearts), the seed that was planted among the thorns (hearts that have worry), and finally the seed that was planted on good soil (hearts open and receptive and believing).

Jesus explains each of these types of soils and what they mean. The seed stolen by the birds is when the devil comes and halts the word of God from being rooted in your heart. It is hard to believe that Satan or the powers of hell may have that authority, but they only have that authority if it is given to them. The way you give them authority is by living a life that is not bent on love and submission to God. You allow compromise into your life, and give satan an open door to remain inside of your heart. Satan is like a lion looking for someone he can devour, and he is looking for any opportunity to get a foothold in your life, to steal, kill, and destroy all things God has for us. Some people have given him that foothold, and have allowed him to latch onto their lives. Some people, maybe it is you yourself, live a life that is okay with evil, and because of that, satan has been stealing your joy, he has been killing your chance to find hope in God, and destroying your worth day by day.

Evil is a strong word, but evil can be so deceiving and disguise itself as a gray area of moral conduct. Satan, in the Garden of Eden did not tempt Adam and Eve with the obvious evil, but he simply tempted them to do what God asked them not to do. Living in disobedience to God and being okay with it gives Satan the authority to take the seed from ever being planted. He has the authority because he has your heart in his hands. If your deepest desires in your heart are just to please yourself, and live a selfish life not concerned for anybody, or you even desire the downfall of others, it is safe to say Satan has your heart. The good news is no matter how deep you are in relationship with darkness (Satan), God has come into darkness to pull you from it; if you will allow Him to. However; if you do not want to leave darkness, then you will remain in darkness.

The heart with the rocky soil represents those who like the idea of who Jesus is, and the life He has to offer, but because life has it's way of hardening our hearts they turn from Him quickly when troubles come. I have known so many people who have fallen into this category, and it is so heartbreaking.

God will move in someone's life and truly reveal just how much He loves them, but unfortunately right after, some hardships will come against them, and they blame God and walk away. They do not realize God did not come to take away all of our problems, but to give us the strength and endurance through His spirit to overcome anything. We have to stop deceiving people by telling them that God is just some magic get out of struggle card. That is not the truth. He has and always will be the one to help us overcome any obstacle. Walking with Christ is a faith journey, through the valleys of death and mountains-tops of joy. It is not just an emotional moment with God that makes everything in life easy. To me that would be cheap love that has no depth if you never have to endure hardship together.

God will be with you comforting you along the way through the hardship. Unfortunately, many do not believe that and go numb to protect themselves from more hurts creating a hard heart.

There is also the seed that is planted among thorns. This is the heart that receives the word of God, but their heart is overwhelmed with worry. Worry is the opposite of faith, and faith is the key to living life with God. So they may grow in knowledge of the truth, but the worries of their heart choke out the fruitfulness of their lives. It is like a plant growing around multiple weeds and weeds overtaking the plant. It had potential, but turns up useless.

Finally the good soil, the soil that receives the love of God, and it completely transforms their lives. They take what they have been given and allow it to shape and grow their lives into something so beautiful and fruitful.

How do we get the good soil? How do we become a soil free from birds(Satan), rocks(becoming calloused), and thorns(worry)? Well, lucky for you I live in the legendary state of North Dakota which is known for its wide vast large farm land. I hear all about the planting process in order to produce good crop. I also worked as a landscaper planting trees and plants, and some of the ground we had to plant on was extremely difficult to maneuver, but we made it work. No matter how many rocks or weeds were in the ground, we worked hard to make it good soil to receive what we were planting, and we can do the same with our hearts. The good news it is never to late to become the good soil. Never to late to soften your heart to receive what God is trying to plant in you. I am not promoting a works-based salvation, but rather God has given us sovereignty over our heart to choose what we allow into it.

The first thing you have to do is to take your life back from Satan, and come to the honest conclusion that it is not okay to live a life in evil and doing wrong. That is the work of the Holy Spirit to convict you of your wrong doings and show you there is something wrong with the way you live, and to show you the way to a better wholesome life out there for you. You cannot be in the grips of Satan and be content, and expect to receive from God well. You have to tell God that you are sorry for living life in evil and tell Him your heart belongs to Him now. He will gladly take over your heart and push all the evil out of it. He will run the birds off that are trying to steal from you.

When it comes to the rocky soil, you have to do what is called rock picking. Rock picking is what farmers do every year before planting season, they work hard to remove all the rocks from the fields that naturally seem to just accumulate over time. I would go rock picking, and it is grueling work. It is hot, your back will start to hurt from lifting all the heavy rocks from the area.

I can relate this to when life throws you a curveball. When tragedy strikes or heartbreak happens. Hardship starts to accumulate naturally, and in this life it is guaranteed. Usually hardship causes our hearts to harden, and the easy thing to do is shut down and numb your heart to protect yourself from more pain.

I have been known to do it, but I'm pleading with you no matter the hurts in your life do not harden your heart towards God, and this takes work. It takes spiritual, prayerful work to come before God and give Him your wounded heart, and allow Him to pick up the rocks to keep your heart open and soft to Him. It's like any relationship. Sometimes it takes effort not to become bitter towards one another, and if any relationship is worth working for, it is your relationship with God. When you remain tenderhearted towards God, it really sets up an opportunity for Him to plant something beautiful within you.

Lets talk about worry. Worry is a killer for so many. Worry is so strongly associated with fear, and fear is so strongly associated with a lack of trust. The reason people have so many business ideas that may be started, but never see the light of day is because they do not have what it takes to trust that it will work out. They worry that there is not enough resources, the timing isn't right, they worry about not being capable, or they are going to be judged and talked about, and they listen to the doubts of others around them.

Same thing goes for our spiritual life. We allow the physical surroundings to dictate what can and cannot happen in our spiritual lives. God may call somebody to go overseas and start a orphanage for those in need. They have been called to change the atmosphere from an abandonment atmosphere, to the atmosphere of a loving family. That person may know that is what God has told them to do, but all the person can see is the lack of money. All the person can hear is the doubt coming from their family and friends. It is not logical or reasonable, so the person never goes. Those orphans never find a home, and continue to struggle on the streets. The worries prohibited something beautiful from taking place. It happens all to often.

These worries are like weeds contaminating and poisoning the process. So what do you do with any weed in a garden? You pull it out! It has no place in the garden. You have to pull the worry from your life, and pull it out by the roots so it will not return again. What is the root of a worry? A lack of trust in God. Allow God to get to the root of your distrust, and allow Him to remove it. Allow Him to win your trust.

All these things are necessary to keeping a heart that is ready to receive what God is trying to do in us. We have to be good groundskeepers of our heart. Groundskeepers are not afraid to get dirty in order to make things ready. When involving matters of the heart it may get messy, but it is well worth it. When Satan tries to steal something from you; you run those birds off and do not let him get a single seed. When life becomes hard you have to pull the rocks out of the way, even though it may seem exhausting, you must keep your heart soft towards God. When weeds begin to pop up from the ground quickly uproot them. You have to proclaim the goodness of God over your worries, and watch them begin to disappear.

This all stems from one important thing. Belief.

You believe God has something for you, and it is not worth allowing Satan to steal it. You believe, even though life is hard, God is going to be with you through the pain. You believe that even if the circumstances do not match up, you serve a God who is capable of the impossible. Therefore; worry will not overtake you, because you have the sweet assurance God will make it happen.

You want good soil? It's simple, believe in the seed that was planted. Believe in Jesus, and don't stop, and through your belief something beautiful in you will be produced. Through your belief, life will begin to grow from the core of your being. Forming you into a tree that displays the life, love, creativity that God has placed in each of those who believe. It truly is that simple. It all starts from believing and it ends in believing.

> " For God so loved the world he gave his one and only son, that whoever BELIEVES in him shall not perish, but have everlasting life." John 3:16

Not earn or deserve, but believe. Belief will be the driving force behind your action. If you have a hard time believing, give your unbelief to God, and allow Him to grow your belief in Him. Every time it feels like I can not really believe what God has said, I will tell Him, and ask Him to change that, and He does, because He is a miracle working God.

Some of you may worried that you have one of the hearts mentioned that do not produce fruit. I have had that concern to. One of things God is willing to do is to give you a new heart if you would receive it. He may give you a brand new heart, He also may make your heart new one day at a time. Trust Him with your heart and watch fruit begin to grow from your heart!

WATER

Christ is the seed, belief is the source of good soil, and water is what is needed to make the seed grow. Water is the source of all life. Without water there is no life. We as humans are made up of 75% water, and the earth's surface is covered by 75% water. Water is so important to our overall physical health and can help play a role in our mental health. I have some friends who really stay on my case about drinking water. There names are Shannon and Olivia. I drink a lot of Mountain Dew and it concerns them. They have this very strong belief, with reason, that if you have any sort of inconvenience it is because you are not drinking enough water. You have a headache? You are not drinking enough water. Feeling lethargic? You did not drink enough water. Your dog ran away? It is because you did not drink enough water!

Alright, the last one I am pulling your leg, but actually Shannon and Olivia have a point. Water really does help with headaches and energy levels. It is also safe to say, wherever water is that is where the life is, and the sustaining of life. Think of a desert without a drop of water. That doesn't exactly depict the image of life, but think of a forest with a flourishing river near. The grass and trees will be green, and animals will reside along the river. Water is a necessity for survival, and for a thriving life environment. Whole communities will migrate and revolve their life around fresh water sources, because where water is there is life and the sustaining of life.

What is the water that our soul needs to grow into a tree? To sustain us in our spiritual walks? We need spiritual water. It may seem like I am always pointing back to Jesus, and that is because I always am! He is the answer to what our soul needs.

When Jesus died on the cross, you can find in scripture that the guards went to check to see if He was dead, they took a spear and pierced it into his side. " He was pierced for our transgressions." Isaiah 53:5. When they did this, it is said that blood and water flowed from His side. I felt the Lord speak to me one day when I truly felt like giving up on the process of becoming a tree. He reminded me of the blood and water that flowed from the sacrifice of Christ. I said, "okay, what does that even mean?" He told me that His blood was the atonement and His grace being poured out for me so that I could have forgiveness. Then He said it wasn't just blood that poured out, but there was water too. He said the sacrifice He gave was enough to forgive me and sustain me. The Blood is the covering, and the water is the sustainer. His life paid for our sins, and His graceful spirit will sustain us. It all comes from one place. The foot of the cross where Jesus poured out His life and spirit for us to be planted and watered into His image. If you feel like giving up, look to the cross, for it has all you need to press on forward.

Jesus talks to a woman at a well and told her, "I will give you living water, that you will never thirst again." Jesus is promising to meet our need for spiritual sustenance. This water is not actual physical water, but spiritual water. Jesus was talking about His Spirit. We need God's spirit to sustain us, we have to have it, the same way our physical bodies need water to sustain living. This is where personal connection comes in. We have to have God's spirit continue to flow through us like a river. Psalms 1 tells us that a man who meditates on God's word is like a tree planted next to a river. He has a constant source of life, for he is near to the river. We must be planted near God's Spirit if we want the spirit life to continue to flow through our being.

This is so crucial for our Christian walk. I feel like Christians walk around spiritually dehydrated. They feel lethargic, and exhausted in their walks. If they feel this way it is because they are not meditating on the word of God. You have no intimate one on one time with Him. You are not planted near the river, for you spend no time in personal prayer, and you wonder why you feel lifeless. It is because your source of water has run dry. You planted yourself in a desert instead of near the river, and that is why you are parched and in desperate need for a sip of God's spirit. I do not mean this in a condemning way, but I am shocked with how many people have been in Christ, but they cannot remember the last time they have spent more then 10 minutes in prayer talking with Him. I am shocked with myself that I have an opportunity to speak to the Maker of all of the universe everyday, the source of refreshment, and sometimes I get lazy with it.

Why cut yourself from our source of energy? To put it plainly, it is pretty stupid. We need that time. Not just for our own sake, but the sake of others. We have the chance to dive right into a river of the presence of an almighty loving God. Let's indulge ourselves in His presence, and watch our energy and livelihood begin to explode.

To put it practically, the days that I spend time with God in authentic worship, prayer, or reading His word my days go a lot better. My energy levels are higher, my attitude is better, and it begins to show that I have been in the presence of God, and drinking of the water my soul needs.

Intimacy with God's spirit is the oil to keep the engine going. It is the drink of water after a long hot journey in the sun. Intimacy, or time spent with anyone is going to lead to a healthy relationship. It is no different for our walk with God. The lovely part about God is spending time with Him should not drain us, but rather fill us up.

The loveliest part of it all is if you feel like you are in a dry season, and feeling desperate for the spirit of God to pour out on you to refresh you, He is waiting for you to ask. Do you feel like your in a desert far from water? Good news! We serve a God who is known to provide water in the driest of places. He made water come from a rock in the days of Moses. He said He will cause water to flow over the mountains. What seems impossible, or so far out of reach is not impossible for God. If intimacy seems out of reach for you, you are wrong and God is waiting to water you into the tree you are designed to become. Sustaining you in your walk with Him and through life, but it all comes from being planted near the river. Walking humbly and enjoying His presence.

> "Come, all you who are thirsty, come to
> the waters; and you who have no money,
> come, buy and eat! Come, buy wine and
> milk without money and without cost."
> Isaiah 55:1

The invitation is before you, and it is free of charge. Christ's Spirit, is the source of water you have been longing for. He is your source of strength, energy, and hope. I cannot tell you enough how many times I have cut myself off from the river, and it begins to drain me. My time with Christ is what sustains me, and will sustain those who love Him.

I challenge you with this; The seed is there, but where is the state of your heart? Are you ready to receive and believe? What is your water intake like? Has your time with God been cut short leaving you dehydrated, or is your heart full of belief, because your time with God so beautiful it is the life within you? These are the thing that will push you to be the "tree" you are destined to be.

> "He asked me, 'Son of man, do you see this?" Then he led me back to the bank of the river. When I arrived there, I saw a great number of trees on each side of the river. He said to me, "This water flows toward the eastern region and goes down into the Arabah, where it enters the Dead Sea. When it empties into the sea, the salty water there becomes fresh. Swarms of living creatures will live

wherever the river flows. There will be large numbers of fish, because this water flows there and makes the salt water fresh; so where the river flows everything will live. Fishermen will stand along the shore; from En to En Eglaim there will be places for spreading nets. The fish will be of many kinds—like the fish of the Mediterranean Sea. But the swamps and marshes will not become fresh; they will be left for salt. Fruit trees of all kinds will grow on both banks of the river. Their leaves will not wither, nor will their fruit fail. Every month they will bear fruit, because the water from the sanctuary flows to them. Their fruit will serve for food and their leaves for healing.'" Ezekiel 47:6-12 NIV

Lastly, give yourself time to grow. You cannot force growth; God is the one that makes it happen. Trust in His ability and His timing.

Chapter 4

TREES AMONGST GRAVES

I am sure some of you are wondering why the name of this book is "Trees Amongst Graves", and if you are not, I am going to tell you anyways.

Just a few months ago I was asked to oversee a funeral of someone I never officially met.Let just say His name was Paul(not his real name), and the only time I saw him was in a hospital bed, and he was asleep. Since he was asleep, I went to go visit his mother who was also in the hospital. His mother is very old, and has a hard time remembering things, but she had an association with the church I worked at in North Dakota. My board thought it would be a good idea for me to go visit them. So I went and talked with her for an hour about various things, prayed for her, and left.

About a week later I got a phone call from someone telling me that Paul had passed away, and for whatever reason they had me in mind to do his funeral for them. Me, a twenty-two year old punk pastor who never even officially met Paul. I was honored and I took the opportunity to hopefully give Paul the honor he deserved. I did not know Paul very well, so I gave a short message about loving the ones around us now, and preached Jesus and the hope we have because of Him.

The funeral went smoothly, and shortly after we went to the grave site. It was a small, middle of nowhere, cemetery. There were maybe 30 gravestones in this particular cemetery, and there was nothing in sight within 15 miles. It was an isolated, windy, and a little overcast day. The family gave their last words, and we lowered Paul into his grave.

After the ceremony, I stuck around to be there to talk to anyone who may have needed it, and a fellow pastor was chatting with another older gentleman next to me. They began to talk about one tree that sat in the middle of the cemetery. Suddenly a wave of revelation hit me, an overwhelming sense came over me that I was supposed to be there at this particular time to see this one tree amongst the graves. Instantly I was inspired. The phrase, "Trees Amongst Graves" came to mind.

I knew it was God-given idea, and I had to figure out what I was going to do with it. Was I supposed to preach a sermon on it and call it good? Or was there more? I knew there was something to this, and finally God let me know I was supposed to write a book on it. I am not a writer, but here I am writing a book that genuinely feels like it was downloaded in my head overnight. All because I went to visit a hospital one afternoon.

It is always cool to see how God will bring things together, and I just wanted you to know where this idea came from before I jumped into it. I also wanted you guys to get the image of what I was seeing at the cemetery, with the one tree in the middle of the graves, and now that you have that image in your head, I want you to keep it in mind as we continue to talk about what it means.

What does it actually mean to have "trees amongst graves"? To be amongst, means to be around to be near, and to be present. In this case, the "Trees" I am talking about are those who are alive, being around those who are dead in their graves. "Trees" are alive in spirit, alive in mind, and alive in heart. These are the people who are sure of who God is, and they can break atmospheres of darkness by just being there. These people can be hidden and surrounded by those who may be breathing, but are dead on the inside in their spiritual graves.

If you look around it is easy to find those who are not truly living, and those who exist without knowing their purpose. This is not a judgmental thing, but so many people actually feel this way. They find it so hard to find true life within themselves, and it is unfortunate. It is a sad reality that I desire no one to be in, but it is the harsh truth of the world we live in. It is difficult to find hope in this life. Though there seems to be a lot of people in despair, I truly believe, amongst the mass amounts of people in their graves, God will also plant at least a "Tree" among them. One person with hope, and life, and He does it all for a purpose.

PLANTED AMONG A CEMETERY

This is a challenge to those who are alive. To those who are trees. To those who are rooted in Christ Jesus, and claim to have life through Him. He has called us to be among those who are dead. He has called us to be among the sinners, the broken, the needy, and the hopeless people of the world. When Jesus planted us in this world, He did not just do it so we would just be alive for our own benefit. He brought us to life for a purpose. He did it so we would be His representation of true life to those in the grave.

We must not separate ourselves into a holy forrest of other trees when there are still many around us in the grave. God is sending us to places that seem like spiritual cemeteries, so that we can be among those in the grave, to love them, and to care for them. We are to walk with those who are in desperate need of life. We are to cherish them even though they may be different then us.

The cemetery that God has planted you in could be your job site, where everyone there is searching for something they cannot seem to find. It could be the classroom full of students who need to receive love. It could be the bar, or the clubs that God has called you to go spread the love of Christ. It could be your local church where Christians are not walking in the abundant life, but Christ has planted you right in the middle of it to spark a sense of revival. Wherever you are, God divinely put you there for a reason.

His sovereignty has placed you to be with the broken, to serve the prideful, and to love the sinners. He placed you among them to love them the way Christ loves them, and we should not stop, no matter the way we are looked at or treated. I am so tired of Christians and churches so bent on being different from those in the grave that they exclude themselves from them. Can't you see, you were once one of them? Can't you see, they are still adored in their grave by Jesus? Can't you see, Jesus looked at you in your grave and came to live among you?

Jesus came for the sick, and the messed up people of this world. When He came to earth He was basically one giant tree, in the midst of tombs, and while He was here He did not reject them, or avoid them to keep from getting dirty. However; He instead ate with them, He cried with them, walked among them, and lived among them.

Let me take this a little further; Matthew 27 takes us to the scene of the crucifixion. The atmosphere was fueled with hate, blasphemy, verbal and physical abuse. The place Jesus carried His cross to is literally called Golgotha "place of the skull". If that isn't the picture of death I do not know what is, and that is right where God planted Jesus. Right in the middle of it... on a cursed tree... *Jesus crucifixion was the first tree among the graves..*

Jesus said If you want to follow him you must deny yourself and pick up your cross... following Jesus often means being planted in dark hard places with hard people. It can be excruciating, but you may be right where God wants you, so that life may come through you.

One of my favorite things to do each year is to go down to Mardi Gras for a missions trip. I team up with Saints Community Church down in New Orleans, during the biggest party of the year, with one mission in mind. To love the people God has called us to love.

On the streets there are people who are drunk, high, homeless, yelling profanities, and partying like crazy. There are homosexuals, witches, and naked people. For your typical church going Christian this would be the last place you would think another Christian should be. We are supposed to avoid such things right? Yeah, we are supposed to avoid behaviors, but not people. The difference is we do not go to join in their lifestyle, but we go to bring life to people on the streets with the love of God. We remain in the world, but not of the world.

Every year there are stories told of God performing miraculous healings on the streets where bars and gay strip clubs surround us. Drug dealers are getting the chance to experience Jesus and His love. I wish some people could experience what it looks like when people with crazy, unexpected backgrounds are told God loves them. God moves powerfully through this, because we are being the image of Jesus on earth. We are His ambassadors, because we are loving the unlovable.

In my experience of walking with God, there are two places where I experience God's presence and power so wonderfully. The first place is the gathering of His people to worship Him. When we gather together and just pour out our adoration for Him, His presence descends on us, and it is so beautiful and peaceful. There is power when the saints join together to adore the One that made them saints. The second place I see God pour out His Spirit is when His saints (trees), go where no one else would go to share this love and life they have received from Him. When the "trees" determine within themselves nothing is going to stop them from loving those in the grave, God is with them and He smiles on them.

Imagine if our churches were set on these two things. To worship God, and the going to bring more people from their graves to join in the worship of God. Knowing full well the only difference between those in the grave and those who are "trees" is the "trees" have come to know the love Christ.

Imagine, if Christians were unafraid to go the house of drunkards, and have dinner with them. Imagine, if Christians were unafraid to speak life over people they work with. Imagine, young high school students fully alive in Christ, sharing the gospel with the students around them who desire suicide. Imagine, speaking to your parents who you know have no true life within, and because you shared with them the key of life, they are changed dramatically. If we did this, we would see the miraculous activity of God in our own homes and neighborhoods The same activity that is already going on all over the world. We would see neighborhoods transformed from spiritual cemeteries to life giving forests of beauty. We would begin to see the omnipresence of God.

One of the biggest turn offs for people coming to Christ is the people who claim to be in Him have no desire to be around them. They think because the people of God do not want to be around them, they assume God himself does not want to be around them. Let's change that. Let's be different. Let's be trees amongst the graves for God's purpose. Let's be great ambassadors of God that reflect His heart directly. Do not settle for being only among other trees at ease, but let us plant ourselves where it is needed the most. Stretch out beyond your typical friend group, and find someone you know needs some life.

The church of Jesus is not confined within temples, or your local church. Jesus will make His church in a Taco Bell at 11 A.M. when a young man prays for someone who has just been in a motorcycle accident. Jesus will make His church on the streets of downtown Chicago, where gang members reside. Jesus will make His church in the homes of the elderly. Jesus will make his church right in the middle of terrorist group. Jesus will make His church wherever His people will go. We are the church. We should be alive and active the same way Christ is alive and active.

Can I be honest? I am so tired of churches thinking everyone is going to just walk through the doors of the church to be reached with this love of God. That is ridiculous. That happens sometimes, but we would see much more fruit if we went out to find the lost.

If I wasn't following Jesus I would be no where near a church, or have any desire to go near one. I am just being honest. What we need is business leaders, teachers, and welders to go into their workplace and begin to come against death, and bring life. Bring life to your environment. No matter how dark and gloomy it may be, Christ planted you in the middle of it to hopefully completely change the landscape of the spiritual climate around you.

TANGIBLE LOVE (I DO CARE)

Something I have experienced in my life as someone who has been following Christ for a few years now is that I do care. I care about those who are not alive in Christ. I desire for them to know this abundant life, and my heart yearns for them to experience the love that pulls them from their grave. I imagine, if I was to ask most church going Christians, all of them, or at least most would say they do care about people who are lost, and dead in their sins. It has been placed within our spirits to care. I have heard so many different messages about going out to the streets and loving people, and my heart gets so inspired by it, but I do not always know how to put what is in my heart to physical tangible action. I think most can relate. Deep down, we care in our spirit, but we can not find a way to unleash what is happening in our spirits into the physical world.

We hope people will come to find they are loved in their spirit by God, but unfortunately people do not work that way. They do not usually just come to recognize they are loved by Christ just over night. I have heard of Muslims who have had dreams of Christ, but they have no one in the real world to tell them, or show them this love they have seen in their dreams, so they never make the choice to follow Jesus.

What I am trying to get at here is people want to feel love, they want something tangible and real that they can take a hold of. In this world before people can experience the love that comes through faith that they can sense in their spirit, they have to see it and feel it. The same way Thomas from the Bible wanted to put his hands in the side of Christ, where Jesus was pierced. He wanted to put his fingers in the holes of His hands of the resurrected Jesus before he would believe Christ was actually risen from the dead. Jesus allowed Thomas to touch His wounds, and Thomas came to believe it was really Jesus and He has risen again. Thomas needed some proof. God has called us to be the proof of His existence and immense love.

Most Christians know without faith it is impossible to please God, and faith is the assurance in things unseen, but normal people do not know that. Christians know that faith in the unseen is what unlocks the love and power of God. Normal people do not know that, they want to see a hands on display of God's love, and God has chosen us to be those hands.

> "Dear friends, since God so loved us, we also ought to love one another. No one has ever seen God; but if we love one another, God lives in us and His love is made complete in us." 1 John 4:11-12 NIV

When Christ came to earth He came to be a physical representation, an ambassador, of the love of God. The way He first began showing the world He loves us is by laying His hands on them and taking away their sicknesses. He was tangibly present, loving His people in word and in action. He did this to open a door to their souls. He did this for them to recognize what happens in the physical is what is truly going on in the spiritual.

Therefore; if you love someone in the physical world, like giving them food to eat, taking care of their children, helping them with their chores, complimenting them, showering them in encouragement, washing their feet, serving them, or being present with them when they lose someone they love, your physical actions speaks to their soul that they are loved.

It is not enough to sit in a church service and sense that you love all of God's people. If you love them, show them!

> "Dear Children, let us not love with words or speech but with actions and in truth." 1 John 3:18.

It is time to take the love God is stirring inside of us for His people, and make it a reality in our lives. This is something I have to remind myself; I can tell people I love them, I love them, I love them, but if I never act on it, it proves to be useless. Words are cheap people. It is easy to say I will be praying for you, but it takes a commitment to that statement to actually take time to lift that person up in prayer. God is waiting on His people who are alive in spirit to make the love manifested in them, to be manifested in those around us. Call that person, tell them you love them, and don't just assume they know you do. Give your extra burger to the homeless guy on the street, not just think about it. Actually give it to him.

For those who are spiritually eager, lay your hands on the sick and allow the Holy Spirit to work through you, and pray for healing and watch God's tangible presence bring healing to their bodies. Do not just desire for God to heal them, step out and at least give God the opportunity to do something amazing.

Desire is crucial. We have to absolutely make our desires that of God's first, but to many people leave it just as a desire, and do not make it a reality. Let us love tangibly. When we decide to love tangibly, it shows the dead, we are really among them, because we love them and more importantly, God loves them.

Chapter 5

ROOTS
(WHO YOU ARE)

In order to be effectively and tangibly loving those who are in their grave, we have to know who we are. So who are you? What would define yourself as? What adjectives would you use to describe yourself? If it is the first day of class, and you are asked to share something interesting about yourself what would you share? If you are like most people, you despise when you have to get up in front of people and explain in just a few seconds who you are. One of the questions that is usually asked during an interview that I loathe is, "can you tell me about yourself Andrew?" It freezes me. I do not know how to explain myself in a way that makes you want to hire me. Do I tell them, "well, my name is Andrew, and I like garlic bread."? Or do I go deeper and give them my ambitions hopes and dreams? Or the labels others have put on me?

For example, right now if I was asked the same question I would say, "yeah, I am a Pastor at church, I am trying to be an author of a book." blah blah blah and so on. But is that what I am? Am I a pastor? Or is that what I do? If I worked as a waiter, astronaut, construction worker, or teacher is that all that I am? Or is there more depth to each and every one of us that is more than just what we do? I personally believe whatever it is that we do comes from who we truly are. What we become in life is just an outward representation of what we believe we are on the inside.

I would say what we do is like the part of the tree that is above ground; the stump, branches, and the fruit that we produce. A tree can produce the most amazing fruit, but that fruit truly comes from the roots that are hidden underneath the surface, and roots come from a seed. We all have our roots. Our roots are our home base, and the basis of who we are.

I think we get so caught up in what we do here on earth, that we think that is what defines us, but can I suggest it is our roots that truly define us? I think many people try to define themselves by their career, or their hobbies, but you have so much more to you than that. I want to remind you, or tell you what your roots are if you are walking in Christ. I want to tell you how He defines you, who you truly are at your core, and how your core defines what you produce in this life.

I am so excited for this Chapter, because this is going to be the most encouraging one. It is so awesome to share with people who God says they are. I personally believe that the number two life-changing experience in a person's life is figuring out who they are, the first being an encounter with The Father, Son, and the Holy Spirit.

KNOWN

The first thing you are is known. You are known. Not just known by your parents, your best friend, neighbors, or your cat. No, you are known by the Almighty, all powerful, all knowing, Creator of the universe. Why is this important? Because I feel like so many people are so unaware of this fact. Either people are unaware, or they have come to the belief that there may be a higher power out there, but He has no involvement with human life. That could not be farther from the truth. We have a God who is so involved, ever present, never forsaking, and knows His creation deeply and intimately. I feel Psalm 139:1-18 would be able to explain just how well known you are better than I ever could.

"You have searched me, Lord, and you know me. You know when I sit and when I rise; you perceive my thoughts from afar. You discern my going out and my lying down; you are familiar with all my ways. Before a word is on my tongue you, Lord, know it completely. You hem me in behind and before, and you lay your hand upon me. Such knowledge is too wonderful for me, too lofty for me to attain. Where can I go from your Spirit? Where can I flee from your presence? If I go up to the heavens, you are there; if I make my bed in the depths, you are there. If I rise on the wings of the dawn, if I settle on the far side of the sea, even there your hand will guide me, your right hand will hold me fast. If I say, "Surely the darkness will hide me and the light become night around me," even the darkness will not be dark to you; the night will shine like the day, for darkness is as light to you. For you created my inmost being; you knit me together in my mother's womb. I praise you because I am fearfully and wonderfully made;

your works are wonderful, I know that full well. My frame was not hidden from you when I was made in the secret place, when I was woven together in the depths of the earth. Your eyes saw my unformed body; all the days ordained for me were written in your book before one of them came to be. How precious to me are your thoughts, God! How vast is the sum of them! Were I to count them, they would outnumber the grains of sand— when I awake, I am still with you." Psalm 139:1-18 NIV

You are telling me that this God who formed galaxies with the word of His mouth knows you, and loves knowing you? There are 8 billion people on earth right now, and it is estimated 108 billion people have lived at some point, and yet God still knows you inside and out. He knows all the hurts you and I have within. He knows the things that bring you joy. He knows the things that you love. He knows your flaws. He knows your weakness and your strengths. He even knows what cereal you like to eat. All there is to know about you, you cannot hide it from Him. You're like an open book before Him. He formed you in His very hands, and He knows you better than you know yourself. It does not matter who you are. You could be Lebron James, or you could be a homeless orphan without a name, and He still knows you. He numbers the hairs on your head.

You may feel overlooked by so many, but it really should not matter, because the Lord knows you. He takes a personal liking to you. You're His creation, His masterpiece. Why else would you spend so much time knowing somebody if you did not value you them immensely? I do not really know much about caterpillars. Why? Because I do not care about them. The things you care about are the things you take the time to get to know. This is who you are. Known and cared for. Simple, but true.

This should change the way you see yourself. If you know you are worth being known by God, the most beautiful being, you could not help but have a sense of self worth. If you know you are known you can overcome feeling overlooked by others. Others may say you are not worth getting to know, but God says you are everything He loves to know.

LOVED. PASSIONATELY.

This brings me to the second root of who you are. The whole reason for your existence. You are loved. I said it earlier in this book, but the only way you can be truly be loved is to be truly known. When you start a relationship or friendship, it is pretty easy to be enamored by the outside and obvious features of a human being. It would be easy to say, "Yes, I love that they are good looking, have a sense of humor, and like sports." I would say that is love, but not passionate love. Until you know someone's flaws and still can say you love them, then you truly love them. No one knows you better than God, and so it must be said that God loves you more than any other thing on this earth ever could.

We hear " God loves you" so often sometimes we do not really appreciate the extent of the truth of that statement. We nullify the love of God so much as human beings, but I just want to refresh myself and all of us with just how passionate and personal this love is. Did you know Jesus often refers to us as His bride? I do not know If you have ever been in love, or married, but Jesus compares His love for us, to that of the love shared between a bride and groom. Do you know how intimate that is? That is not a far-off, cold hearted God but rather He is a

God who is tenderhearted towards His lovers. The book Song of Songs in the Bible, is a group of poems between two lovers. We usually try to avoid this book, because it talks about breasts and it's weird, but the reason it is in the Bible, I would assume, is because God is showing us the way He feels about us through the intimacy this couple shows each other.

Song of Songs Chapter 3, speaks of a woman who cannot find rest, because she is longing and yearning for her lover. She misses him. Have you ever experienced this? Have you ever missed someone enough that it kept you up at night? This woman cannot get enough of him. She is intoxicated by him. When he is not around, she gets up out of bed to go on the search for him. Get up out of bed?! She must be in love. She compares her lover's love to being sweeter than wine, and wine is a symbol of joy throughout the Bible. For whatever reason, she is so thrilled by the love of this man she claims his love is better than joy itself, and the man feels the exact same way. Song of Songs is a pretty intimate book, but that is because Jesus is an intimate God. You know Jesus gets thrilled just by our presence?

I had a friend in high school that said once, " Sisk, I heard you were coming, and dude I got all giddy." Shout out Landon. I felt so valued by that statement, and that was an imperfect flawed human being. Christ, a perfect being, feels that way on a consistent basis for us, and on a higher level. It literally does not make sense, but for whatever reason it does not stop Him from loving. What do we have to offer Him? Not much, but because we belong to Him, He loves us with such passion. He loves us like a young groom watching his new bride walking down an aisle, and His heart jumps within Him. God's heart jumps within Him when He thinks of you, and He is always thinking of you. A million thoughts of you flood his mind every moment.

> "Place me like a seal over your heart, like a seal on your arm; for love is as strong as death, its jealousy unyielding as the grave. It burns like blazing fire, like a mighty flame. Many waters cannot quench love; rivers cannot sweep it away. If one were to give all the wealth of one's house for love, it would be utterly scorned." Song of Songs 8:6-7 NIV

I could tell you countless times I have felt unloved, unwanted, not worthy of God's love, and still He pours His love out on me. Holding nothing back. I remember one time I was feeling down in the dumps, deep in insecurity and self-hate, and I happened to be reading Psalm 45:1-3 (NLT).

> "Beautiful words stir my heart. I will recite a lovely poem about the king, for my tongue is like the pen of a skillful poet. You are the most handsome of all. Gracious words stream from your lips. God himself has blessed you forever. Put on your sword, O mighty warrior! You are so glorious, so majestic!"

After reading this I felt the Lord say to me so gently, "Andrew, this is how I feel about you." What?! God why? I did not understand, but I trusted it. It brought me to tears that even though I have so many weakness He still thinks this about me. This is the praise He should be receiving! He should be told He is a handsome mighty warrior! Yet He casts it on a lowly sinner like me. The reason I share this personal story is because I have a personal love relationship with Christ, and each and everyone of us can too. It is who you are. Loved passionately. Imagine what it would look like if we walked around knowing this to be true. The confidence we would have, the joy we would have would be too much to contain.

The problem is people do not think the Jesus wants to be around them, or is pleased to be with them. Well the truth is that the same pleasure the Father found in Jesus "this is My beloved Son whom I love, with Him I am well pleased" (Matthew 3:17), is the same pleasure, and approval that has been passed down to us by faith in Jesus. When we put our faith in Jesus He gave us everything that belonged to Him, and that was the love, approval and pleasure the Father had in Him. The Father is happy, glad, delighted, gratified, grateful, thankful, thrilled, elated, proud especially so to walk with you in Love.

A FORGIVEN SON OR DAUGHTER

One of the most powerful forces on this earth is the power of forgiveness. It has the power to break strongholds, the power to set free, the power to heal the wounds of a relationship, and reconcile the most hated of enemies. It allows love to come in and replace the hurt. It can cause transformation within a person, especially when forgiveness is undeserved, but is given anyways. It has the power to completely change one's path of life.

We all have made decisions in our life that we regret. We have done things to hurt other individuals and ourselves. We have all at one point have gone against God. Most humans on this earth can recognize they are not perfect and made mistakes. We carry these failures in our soul, and some understand that, and feel the weight of their guilt, and it haunts them. Others may feel it, but they find no remorse for their actions. Just because you ignore it, does not make it go away.

This is the beauty of the gospel; Christ came to bring forgiveness to all of mankind. Forgiveness according to ole reliable Wikipedia says:

> "forgiveness is the intentional and voluntary process by which a victim undergoes a change in feeling and attitude regarding an offense, lets go of negative emotions such as vengefulness, forswears recompense from or punishment of the offender, however legally or morally justified it might be, and with increased ability to wish the offender well."

When Christ was on earth He encountered so many who were considered the worst kind of people. They had no reason to be forgiven for their actions. They were deserving of punishment from God according to the law. Tax collectors, thieves, prostitutes, adulterers, and murderers. People whom culture deems to far gone to come back from their life of sin, and what does Christ do? He encounters them, and He eats with them. Just by His presence they recognize they have fallen short of being perfectly good. He forgives them, no strings attached and He calls them son and daughters. All of these sinners leave their encounter completely changed by the forgiveness they have received, because they know it is unmerited.

When Jesus was on the cross bleeding out He looked out and said, "Father forgive them, they know not what they do." He looks to those who have committed an offense against him (they literally put him to death for no good reason) and He not only forgives them, but He also prays for our well-being.

All because Christ poured out His life for us, we find undeserved forgiveness of all our wrongdoings. Every sin you have committed that no one knows about is completely washed away by the life that Jesus laid down. Our sin gone and forgotten by God. A clean slate. Our sentencing that we deserved for our sins, He paid for. So God looks at us with complete affection, not remembering our past, present, or future sins. We are blessed, because of this. We are honored, because of this. It is who we are. Forgiven. We live in a state of forgiven. Nothing can change that, not our mess ups, or weaknesses. Even the filthiest of sins is not remembered. Even the sins that are brought up again and again by others are still not remembered by God, because of the superiority of Christ sacrificial love poured on us.

So many people feel they have to flee from God because of their past. They feel it is too dirty, too awful, too evil, but God looks at us now pardoned, righteous, and favorable. This is the truth. I no longer carry the weight of guilt and shame for my sins, because I handed them over to Jesus and He threw them into the sea of forgetfulness, and only God has the power to do that.

One time I was feeling guilty about one of my past sins I had a vision. The worst thing I had ever done was brought back into my mind, replaying itself over and over again in my head. In the vision I saw myself carrying a box, an ugly horrendous black box, and this box was representing my sin. This box looked like it was from the underworld of Stranger Things the Netflix series. I was trying desperately to get rid of it, but it was impossible. Jesus then came walking up to me and said, "Son, give it to me." Reluctantly I gave it to Him; I had no other choice. As I handed it over to Him, Jesus was taken and nailed on a fence post, and the box of sin I handed Him disappeared. It no longer existed. God spoke to me a valuable message to me that day. My most shameful sin was no match for the love and power of Christ.

Now I am no longer identified by my sin, but rather I am identified as blessed. Blessed because I am forgiven. Forgiven to the extent that I am no longer at odds with God, but now He calls me son. He says I am family to Him. I am loved as a son and all that entails, and He calls to me to act as such. He calls me to be someone who acts like their father, and is loved by his father. He does this for me, and He is doing this for all of those who believe in Him.

He did this for a woman in the Bible who had a bleeding issue, which is considered unclean according to the law, and He healed her, because she reached out to Him in faith. He then calls her daughter, a term of endearment. This woman was no longer considered the unclean woman with a bleeding issue, she is now known as the woman who Christ calls daughter. She did not have to clean herself up; she came to Christ as she was, and He transformed her. He did this for the murderer Saul, and transformed him into his Son, who acted like his father by sharing love to all he came across. Saul ended up writing most of the New Testament of the Bible that we have today.

The spirit of Christ does this in prisons, where thieves, murderers, gang members, and the outcasts of society are placed. He infiltrates these prisons and forgives them, even though the state may not. Now, we have convicted felons who are forgiven by God, and He remembers their sins no more. Now, through their forgiveness, their hearts were changed and their status changes from enemies of God to sons and daughters of God. Because their roots have changed they act like sons and daughters of the most loving God. Their hearts are tender, they become servants, and loving people.

That is who you are, if you are in Christ. You are forgiven of any and all sin, small or large, and He adopts you into His family. You are no longer abandoned as an orphan; you now belong. You belong to Him, and you are loved by the King of Majesty, the creator of all things. You are now welcomed into his arms with a hug and kiss. Once we can get this down; once we truly discover who we are, we can act accordingly. When we know we are known we will walk through life as if we are worth knowing, like we have value. When we know we are loved passionately, we will walk in confidence, and in joy that love brings. When we know we are forgiven and part of the family, we are no longer going to walk in shame, but in freedom.

My prayer for each of us, is that we would come to acknowledge the truth of who we are, and that God would show us our roots, and it would be manifested in our lives.

Chapter 6

"ROOTS 'BOUT TO BUST 'EM OUT"

Have you ever seen a tree that has roots so large that they start to work themselves through the ground messing up everything around them? Walking down the streets of New Orleans, the sidewalks begin to crack and deform, because the tree's roots that are planted near grow underneath and break apart the cement.

It makes the the sidewalks insufficient for riding bikes, but it is pretty aesthetically pleasing. These roots begin to change neighborhoods and landscapes. Remember that funeral I was telling you about? I want you to try and picture what the cemetery looked like. Obviously, there were headstones, green grass and one huge tree in the middle. It's roots are coming up out of the ground, and they were pushing up against the headstones. It was obvious these roots were in the ground right next to the coffins.

That is where I heard the phrase come from an older gentlemen's lips, "Roots 'bout to bust 'em out". He was talking about the coffins. It seemed as if these tree's roots were going to break the coffins open. Suddenly an image came to my mind of these roots breaking open the coffins, and the dead that were in them were now set free from their grave, and had the opportunity to live again. It was a powerful and moving sight, because I felt like that is the exact representation of what it ought to be like for those who are in alive Christ Jesus, among those who are dead in their sins. The Trees should be breaking open graves, by saying He forgave me, He loves me, He knows me, and He can do it for you!!

We should be breaking apart the graves our friends live in. We should bust it open with no regard for the coffin. We should be setting free those held captive by death, so that they may walk among the living again and be truly living themselves. That is the heart behind this book. It is to challenge us to bring life where life seems far-gone. To call the living to bring hope where darkness seems to reign.

You and I should be like Ezekiel when God takes him to the valley of dry bones. A place that is lifeless, but as Ezekiel speaks life, the bones in the valley come together and flesh forms over the bones forming them into a life-like body. We should be speaking life, and through the power of God, we will watch the dry bones around us come together and flesh will wrap around them again, and the Spirit of God will breathe into their lungs. Raising them from the dead. All for the purpose of being an army for Him. (Ezekiel 37)

WHEN GOD DISAGREES WITH DEATH

The typical person would say death is the end of it. There is no coming back from death, put the nail in the coffin, and that is the end of that story. Well, I know a God that disagrees with that completely. I know a God whose jealous love is as demanding as the grave. I know a God who calls out to Lazarus, after 4 long days of being confirmed dead, and says "Lazarus, Come out!" (John 11:43) Through the authority of His voice, Jesus speaks to the certainty of death and overwhelms it, and Lazarus wakes up leaving behind his tomb and grave clothes, although it seemed too late. He was dead and gone. Not a chance of breath coming into his lungs again, but God disagreed.

Obviously we know on the third day after His death, Christ rose again from His tomb that was guarded by a giant rock and two Roman soldiers. It seemed like there was no hope of life, but once again God disagreed. When God disagrees there is nothing that can stop Him.

> "I know that You can do all things; no purpose of yours can be thwarted." Job 42:2.

No one can stop Christ's purpose, and Christ's purpose from the very beginning was to bring the spiritually dead back to life again. Oh, and the physically dead as well.

> "And when Jesus had cried out again in a loud voice, he gave up his spirit. At that moment the curtain of the temple was torn in two from top to bottom. **The earth shook, the rocks split and the tombs broke open. The bodies of many holy people who had died were raised to life. They came out of the tombs after Jesus' resurrection and went into the holy city**

and appeared to many people."
Matthew 27:50-53

This is quite the phenomenon, and it is unheard of, but that is what Christ has come to do in this world. To bring those who are walking around in their spiritual grave, to true abundant life. That is His work, and He has called us to take part in that work. It is not to late for anybody or any circumstance when God is present. No matter how far gone you are in the darkness, or how deep in the miry clay you are, the power of His resurrection has the power to make a great comeback from death. It is never too late. No matter who you are, or where you are spiritually, your spiritual death does not have to be the end of your story. If anyone tells you it is too late for you or someone you know, just know God disagrees.

"There is nothing Satan can kill that God won't resurrect"

OUR ROOTS, NOT OUR BRANCHES OR FRUIT.

How are we going to take part in this work? So many of us want to take part in this, but it seems impossible to do so, because it is a supernatural occurrence to bring dead souls to life. We as humans have been trying to figure out the best to way to take part in this work of bringing the spiritually dead to life. We have been trying to figure what technique we can use to pry open these graves.

You see it in churches that try to find strategies to more effectively tell people about the love of Christ in a way that pulls them to life. If we are not careful we will begin to trust in strategies rather than God's Spirit. We think if we can produce the best quality stuff, that will be the thing that will pull people from the grave. I've done it. Sometimes I get caught thinking, if I can be the best pastor around then maybe people will come to know Jesus. As if my success is going to be the answer. I get caught thinking, if I speak sermons that touch the heart and emotions of people, then they will want this thing that I have within me. We think, if we have the best music, then people will like what we produce and they will want what we have inside of us. We think, if we become the most successful business man or woman with countless resources, then maybe we can pull people from their graves. We think, that after we get our lives all together, then maybe we can take part in this work.

We want our strengths, resources, or strategies to be the answer. We don't realize these things are not what we need to break open graves. Our strengths, talents and abilities are not the answer, though they can be tools. Yes, let's become great people, who serve and love strategically, and are successful at what we do, but that is like the leaves, branches, and the fruit of a tree. These things can be beautiful and pleasing and good, as it should be, but it is not in the dirt where people who are dead are located. What we become on the outside is just a blessing for those around us, but it not the thing that will break open coffins.

Our roots; that is how we are going to break open the graves. Remember our roots? The fact that you are known by God, you are loved by God, and you are a forgiven sinner that has become a Son and Daughter of God, only by His grace. We do not need our tactics to try and persuade people into living the Christian lifestyle. Our successes are not even close to the power that we have within our roots. My sermons, which I consider my strength, will not even compare to the power that comes from the fact that God loves me passionately.

The power that is displayed through us with our talents, does not even come close to the power that is within us that comes from just being a simple son and daughter of God.

We must grow as sons and daughters first, and allow the Spirit that Christ placed within us that calls out to Him "Abba" Father. We need His spirit within us to be pushed up against people in their grave. The same Spirit that raises the dead to life.

> "Not by might nor by power, but by my Spirit,' says the Lord Almighty."
> Zechariah 4:6 NIV

Whatever our role is in society it is secondary to what we are at our core. Being a pastor is not going to pull people to the abundant life Jesus purchased. Being a successful person will not pull people to the abundant life Jesus has purchased. Us being down in the dirt with people, loving them with the unimaginable love our Father shows us, and showing them we are just sinners forgiven by the sacrificial love of Jesus Christ, will pull them out. It will raise there faith when they here God did it for us He can do it for them. Sharing from our core the beauty of this free and ever abounding grace is what will 'bust em out'. Your strengths will not cut it, but God's strength in you is the key to busting graves open.

> "But He said to me, "My grace is suffi-
> cient for you, for my power is made per-
> fect in weakness." Therefore I will boast
> all the more gladly about my weaknesses,
> so that Christ's power may rest on me." 2
> Corinthians 12:9 NIV

Allow the Father to teach you to be a son and daughter of His, before you know it you will be walking like Jesus who was Thee Tree amongst the Graves, that busted us out of our spiritual death.

So go! Go on and share this beautiful grace that pulls us from death, and calls us sons and daughters. Allow who God has formed you to be pull others from despair right into the loving arms of Jesus. Continue the work your Father has been doing from the beginning of time, bringing life where there was no life. You do not have to be something extraordinary to do this work, you just have to be His.

We live in a world full of two kinds of people. The ones that feel like they are dying inside, or the ones that walk around with true life flowing from them. In this book we look through some of the characteristics of both the living and the spiritually dead, and what should be the mission of those who are alive and well in a world that seems to be losing life as it goes. Hopefully this will challenge you, encourage you, and draw you closer to Jesus and His purpose for your life.

Author: Andrew Sisk

In Honor of Taylor Bliss & Amelia Speltz